A Danger to Self and Others

Tyree Campbell

**A Danger to Self and Others
by Tyree Campbell**

All rights reserved. No part of this book may be reproduced or transmitted in any form or by any means, electronic or mechanical, including photocopying or recording or by any information storage and retrieval systems, without expressed written consent of the author and/or artists.

A Danger to Self and Others is a work of fiction. Names, characters, places, and incidents are products of the author's imagination. Any resemblance to actual events or persons, living or dead, is entirely coincidental.

Poem copyrights owned by Tyree Campbell
Cover illustration by Sandy DeLuca
Cover design by Laura Givens

First Printing, January 2018
Second Printing 2025

Hiraeth Publishing
P.O. Box 1248
Tularosa, NM 88352
e-mail: hiraethsubs@yahoo.com

Visit www.albanlakepublishing.com for online science fiction, fantasy, horror, scifaiku, and more. Stop by our online bookstore there for novels, magazines, anthologies, and collections. **Support the small, independent press...and your First Amendment rights.**

Introduction

I'm not a poet.

It's not that I don't know how to compose poetry (though some might disagree on that point); I have a third-place Rhysling and several best-of-issues that suggest I can do so rather well. But for me each piece of writing—story, essay, or poem—has a purpose; through it I have something to say, however significant or inane. It might be to express an emotion, such as anger, loss, or outrage; it might be to call attention to some aspect of human existence; it might be to summon the thought processes, to make the reader say, "Huh!" Or perhaps to elicit a smile or a guffaw, both of which appear to be in short supply these days.

So sometimes, when what I want to say can best be said via poetry, I compose poems.

With poetry, less is more. That's why this introduction is so short. However well or poorly, the contents herein speak for themselves . . . and for me.

Tyree Campbell
Tularosa, NM
Spring 2025

Introduction
by Kendall Evans

What is the difference between ordinary poetry and science fiction poetry? The answer to this question can be found in Tyree Campbell's poetry collection, *A Danger to Self and Others*. Science fiction poetry, when it's serious, has the entire cosmos to consider. And when it's playful, it has the entire universe to play with. On the serious side, take a look at Campbell's poem "Evolution," which opens the collection. Or you want playful? Read his poem titled "How the Solar System Really Lost its Tenth Planet," or "Garden Party."

Allow me to clarify – When I speak of science fiction, I'm also talking about fantasy. Both allow the exploration of all Space and Time. Why would anyone ever want to read or write ordinary poetry rather than science fiction and fantasy poetry? I have no idea. Who out there really doesn't want to explore all of all that there it, to ponder it all, question it all, seek to understand it all? Cosmic games are much more fun than games confined to mundane realms.

Take a look at Campbell's wonderful fun on *Homo sapiens* in his poem "Itinerant." Oh, and do you like dragons? (And who doesn't like dragons?) Tyree has a whole section of dragon poems in this collection.

You like short poems? Haiku? Take a look

at what science fiction and fantasy haiku can do, because there's a section of those too in the collection.

Introductions are best left brief, so I will end this here. But don't forget to read my favorite poem in the collection, "Not One of Us," – one of the most poignant fantasy poems I've read in a long time.

    Kendall Evans
    Norwalk, CA
    October 2024

Quantum Women
by Tyree Campbell

A quantum is a self-contained unit—of energy, light, and so forth. It exists in and of itself, irrespective of its surroundings. But it can be, and usually is, part of a team. A quantum woman, then, is a self-contained person, independent, yet willing to be part of a team if the right teammate comes along.

Quantum women aren't superheroines with superpowers, they're not "chicks in chain mail," although they might be, as Pamela Sargent wrote, "Women of Wonder." For the most part, quantum women are everyday folks in a science fiction or fantasy setting. They might be home-makers or home-wreckers, homely or homey, but all of them are focused, determined, willful, and independent. To those who have men in their lives, they are partners and companions, equals and not subordinates.

And yet, like any of us, they can find themselves in extraordinary situations where a bit of heroism can save the day. You'll encounter them on these pages.

www.hiraethsffh.com/product-page/quantum-women-by-tyree-campbell

Contents

science fiction   11

Evolution
Itinerant
Not One of Us
The Last Rub of the Lamp
How the Solar System Really Lost its
    Tenth Planet
The Garden Party
The Last Moon of the Morning

dragons   31

Black Dragon
La Tanière à Minuit
The Lair at Midnight
Midnight Dragons

personal   43

In Memoriam
Auld Acquaintance
Watch Me

darker   49

A Danger to Self and Others
Spellchecker
First Fright
True Reflection
Purrifurry
Me That Was
Bringing Sally Back
Size 15W Should Do It

minimalist   69

Scifaiku
Tanka
Featured Poet: Scifaikuest August 2008

oddments   79

My Grandfather's Corpse

illustrations   57

True Reflection by Marcia A. Borell

science fiction

Evolution

Atom
Molecule
Replication
Virus
Helix
Helices
Troping
Cell
Reproduction
Colony
Differentiation
Organ
Sensing
Clumping
Eeewwww, gross!
Critter
Lung
Crawl
Stand
Tool
Hunt
Think
Gather
Count
Build
Write
Read

Invent
Property
Possess
Own
Acquire
Take
H-Bombs and Rockets and Missiles, oh my!
Atom

Itinerant

the next tree over
lends a view of the plains
what's out there

hunt and gather
settle here and there
oh, look, there's a river
let's follow it

settle here, settle there
move on

a lake, go around it
a sea, cross it
an ocean, explore it
an ice bridge
joins landmasses
to new plains
new rivers
new settlements
moving on

until at last
Hobo sapiens looks up

Not One of Us

He sat down at our table,
    the way starfarers do
Mindful of his balance,
    and careful of his brew
His skin was dark and blistered.
    He sported three tattoos
One on either shoulder,
    in praise of craft and crews
The third we thought said "Mother,"
    in letters black and dead
Honoring his parent,
    on scroll unfurled and red.

Roberto made a gesture,
    and bought a round of drinks.
Danny nudged and nodded,
    and eyed him like a lynx
Awaiting one more victim.
    To pay a gruesome toll
For sitting at our table,
    he'd have to sell his soul.
"What story lies behind it?"
    Old Binjo fin'ly asked,
Yellow forehead wrinkled,
    his left arm in a cast.

"The first and last and only,"
      he said and blew some froth
And white mist slowly fell
      upon the tablecloth.
It rose an apparition,
      and formed a woman fair,
Sapphires filled her eyeholes,
      and onyx bound her hair.
She wore an ancient chiton,
      bright white with purple hem.
On her forehead glistened
      a golden diadem.

"A ghost!" yelled 'Bert, and Binjo
      cried out his protest loud.
The ruckus 'round the image
      began to draw a crowd.
Her voice came soft and distant,
      as if from farthest stars
Fragile as an old wine,
      or chimes of silver bars
"No ghost be I," she whispered.
      My skin began to crawl.
Her sultry voice entrapped us
      in her siren's call

"I am as you now see me,
    a lucent cloud of gas,
Nothing more of substance.
    A stellar chamber lass
Who longs for some man's comfort,
    but cannot feel his touch
Who out there among you
    would understand as much?
For eons I have traveled,
    the last one of my kind
Searching for a lover,
    a kin of my own mind."

"Is it you or you or you?"
    She pointed at each one.
And bade us all approach
    like planets to her Sun
"You cannot grasp my horror,
    to be so long alone
A glove without a hand,
    or flesh without the bone.
One kiss is all I'm asking,
    a touch upon my face."
Indigo from sapphires
    now swept around the place.

Roberto drifted forward,
    his hand reached for her breast.
Its softness now he sought,
    to put her words to test
If touch it was she wanted,
    then touch it was she'd get.
Fingers passed right through her—
    with fear he was beset.
She sucked him full into her,
    and made him disappear.
Old Binjo cried alarm,
    and Danny spilt his beer.

"Free that man," cried Little Van,
    who kept the bar and peace.
Massive shoulders knotted,
    to force 'Berto's release.
The apparition softened,
    and sighed a coffin's sigh
And as Van touched her skin,
    she drank his substance dry.
Another and another
    into the vapor went
Without permit or nod
    or giving their consent

The starfarer sat silent
      and scratched his arm's tattoo
Not a word he uttered,
      nor partook of his brew.
Then Danny swore an oath
      and he fired a candle wick,
Set it underneath her.
      "Now that should do the trick."
But she seemed not to notice
      the flames that licked her mist
Smiled she did at Danny.
      "Come to me, I insist."

"No," cried I, and "No," said he,
      and Binjo said, "Enough.
You have those you came for."
      She bent and touched his cuff.
The plasters weren't organic,
      his body stayed in place.
His eyes rolled dollar slots,
      and Jackpot drained his face
Of color, breath, and humor,
      the things that make us live.
His soul was all she took,
      he'd nothing more to give.

Sapphires locked onto my eyes,
    the next in line I was.
Sorrow overwhelmed her
    as long solitude does.
"You're lonelier than I am,"
    she cried and Binjo's eyes
Reclaimed their vivid hue,
    and canceled his demise.
Your mate departed with your dog,
    she told me in my mind.
Our shared grief has spared you,
    you are of mine own kind.

With that she flowed back to him,
    the 'farer's misty brew.
He downed her with two gulps,
    and scratched his arm anew.
The crowd began dispersing,
    in search of other fare
To stimulate, excite,
    or chill them in this lair.
Interest waned and faded quick.
    The 'farer rose to leave,
While those who'd lost their friends
    now drank a brew to grieve.

His third tattoo said "Other."
    I saw so clearly how
She'd lost her kin in space,
    but she'd replaced them now.
My loneliness had saved me,
    I'd only make her worse.
She dared not take me too,
    and so I write this verse.
Perhaps you think this story
    is false. Well, stay right here.
The Other has fresh souls,
    but she'll be back next year.

The Last Rub of the Lamp

meet me on the corner
of the Universe
where the gray shroud
of the oldest suns
casts from us each and both
the same shadow
and take me and my dreams
where you will

I've been a soldier far too long
against my will
a bootheel trapping
in the recesses of me
that which I was to have been

so near the end now,
these dreams are mine
to keep
to share

come, meet me on
the corner of this Universe
and take me into the next one

How the Solar System Really Lost Its Tenth Planet
[stolen without remorse or shame from "The Night Before Christmas"]

'Twas the late Cenozoic and all through
    the court
Not a juror was stirring [they'd heard it before].
Representative Shmee hung in gibbets
    from where
They envisioned a verdict both partial and fair.

The witnesses came with their testimony
To confirm the verdict irrevocably.
Thumb poised on the button, about to delete,
The judge banged his gavel, and all took a seat.

"An eon you've had," said the judge
    to the Shmee,
"to develop space travel and explore
    what you see.
But you've fought with yourselves
    over which ills to cure,
And which folk to banish to
    make yourselves pure.

"The money you've wrung from your
    resources fair
Was wasted on comforts with nary a care
To your true destiny, which lay in the stars,
Outward past Jup'ter and inward past Mars

"You've exhausted your world -- the Fifth
    as it's known
To those of us watching you reap
    what you've sown.
Your time is now up, and this button I'll thumb
Before you are able to waste one more crumb."

"Wait!" cried the Shmee, protesting this docket.
And one pulled a tattered old book
    from his pocket.
"Just look what we've done," he said,
    fanning the pages
Of history, science, and words from the sages.

"Our everyday dudgeon is eased by machines.
We talk to each other on monitor screens.
We travel on roads—" "All in need of repair,"
said the judge to the Shmee with
    a baleful stare.

"Your destiny's greater than any of you are.
You've squandered it making your planet
    a sewer.
What you do is what counts, and your feelings
    don't matter
To me who's decision ain't based on the latter."

"Wait!" cried the Shmee, "Give us one more
    chance, please!"
"No, the Fifth Planet's sick, and you're all
    a disease,"
said the judge, and he thumbed down the
    button. "That's that.
So much for your chances and your habitat."

To the hypersolarium jurors flew in a flash,
And saw in the holo an orbital gash.
In defense of the Shmee they had said
    not a word.
"Fuck 'em all," shrugged the judge,
    as he turned to the Third...

The Garden Party

"You know it's made us stronger,"
said the weevil to the bee
The butterfly agreed with him,
'Tween bites of broccoli

"The aphids' evolution
And the spiders' victory
deserve a round of heartfelt thanks
and praise in memory."

"We couldna done wi'out them,"
chimed the Scottish termite clan.
"But we've lived longer than they ha',
And we've prevailed again."

"Still 'tis rather sad they're gone"—
The red inchworm's suggestion.
"Their antics when the weeds came up
Aided our digestion."

The caterpillar wandered,
Porting several serving sets,
To offer them refreshments and
Replace the old baguettes.

Before each one she stood up,
asking very courteously,
"More dCon on your kaiser roll?
More Roundup in your tea?"

The Last Moon of the Morning

[with apologies to The Eagles and "Hotel California"]

On a dark Martian highway
At the skimmer controls
Heading for Marineris
In between the two Poles

Drawing near the next crater
I saw a glowing mirage:
A young woman with a warm smile and a fine decolletage

At the entrance she stood straight
Bade me stop and dismount
Led me into the crater
And her spectral redoubt

Then she took off her sandals
And sat down on the sand
Near us stood an ancient tavern and I
Heard a song from the band

Welcome to *The Last Moon of the Morning*
It's the only place
We can stay these days
Few of us left in *The Last Moon of the
        Morning*
Nothing here but the tears
For our yesteryears

I thought I should dock my skimmer
[It's made by Mercedes-Benz]
She made a signal with her hands to
Send out one of her friends

And she sighed like a coffin
Opened for the first time
Clouds of memories escaped her
Without reason or rhyme

'Twas her civilization
Represented in light
Scenes were floating around me
Rising into the night

I saw cities and space ships
All disease was wiped out
Free technological answers
No competition allowed

And here in *The Last Moon of the Morning*
When they gathered here
And they drank their beer
They thought it would last till the last
    moon of the morning
But were they surprised
When the Earth arrived

I saw the coming of Earthmen
The domes and colonies
Terraforming the landscape
With their trash and debris

Soon our oxygen killed them
And our emissions, too
We didn't take the time to know them
And they faded from view

While I watched her she vanished
And the morning came red
The refrain from the tavern
Was the last thing they said

Welcome to *The Last Moon of the Morning*
Since you humans arrived
There's no one else left alive
We're saying goodbye in *The Last Moon
    of the Morning*
Leaving you to think on
What you'll lose when we're gone.

Black Dragon

'Tis a fable that scarcely needs telling
Though it's told oft enough just the same
Of the battle between Good and Evil
And of those who would honor Good's name

How the mighty Saint George slew the dragon
How he saved all of Christendom's souls
But the truth is that George never did it
And the legend is full of huge holes

Like a coin all our stories have two sides
Only winners shall live to tell theirs
If across from the Yang is the Yin, then
Who knows which of them answers the
    prayers?

Ancient Ormazd and Ahriman battled
And if living would fight once again
They'd established a balance between them:
Neither one nor the other should win

As The Light and The Darkness are dual
So the archetypes Evil and Good
Both reflect in our myths and our legends—
Inspiration we take where we would

Who's to say whether George or the dragon
Represents what we cherish or hate?
If beliefs should extol all things human
Then the dragon must suffer its fate

So White Knight and Black Dragon did battle
And the Knight, being White, must have won
Because black is the color of demons
And of those who would hide from the Son

All these years we've condemned all the
    dragons
And heaped all our praise on the knights
But what if the knights upheld Evil
And the dragons had fought for our rights?

Oh, the triumph of Good over Evil
Is the way that we wish it to be
Ah, but how can we know which is which?
Good is Good, Bad is Bad, by decree

Now the priests say some Saints ne'er existed
Save in fables and legends and lores
And Saint George was the merest of figments
Which means the Black Dragon still roars

So if you should awaken 'round midnight
And run hard to your window to see
The Black Dragon you've feared still is out
    there
Yet you sense you're as safe as can be

Because all of the knights of the fables
Now are faded and vanished from view
For the Good has outlasted the Evil
The Black Dragon will watch over you.

La Tanière à Minuit

Par le noir et les ombres
    Ils sont venus
A leur petite place
Entre la nuit et les étoiles

Pendant des siècles il se cherchaient
    Chacun pour l'autre
Ce soir
En fin
Ils se sont trouvés, l'un et l'autre

Ils sont jumeaux de la même âme
    Nés de la même âme
    Nourris de la même âme

Deux memoires anciennes du feu et de la
    fumée
Les derniers dragons

Ce soir leur pensées sont leur espérance
Ce soir leur ardeur est leur feu
    Feu des dragons
    Feu des esprits
Feu de leur seule âme

Revenants anciens sont retournés
Revenants des dragons qui ont passé
Revenants des manières anciennes
    Encore ils renaissent

Les dragons des minuits sont seuls dans cette
    place
Seuls . . . mais
Leur pensées deviennent des idées pour les
    autres
Il y auront plus des dragons, nés d'espérance
    Nés des pensées
    Nés du feu et de la fumée

Ces deux, ils sont retournés
Ils vaincront

The Lair at Midnight

Through the dark and the shadows
    They are come
To their little place
Between the night and the stars

For centuries they have searched
    For one another
Tonight
At last
They have found one another

They are soulmates
    Born of the same spirit
    Nourished by the same spirit
Two ancient memories of fire and smoke
The last dragons

Tonight their thoughts are their hopes
Tonight their love is their fire
Dragon's fire
Dragon's spirit
Fire from the same soul

Old ghosts are returned
Ghosts of other dragons who have passed on
Ghosts of the old ways
    Once more reborn

The dragons of midnight are alone in this place
    Alone . . . but
Their thoughts sustain others
There will be other dragons, born of hope
    Born of ideas
    Born of fire and smoke

These two are back
The dragons will win

Midnight Dragons

minuit
the darkest hour for most
the brightest hour for them
they are stirring
she in her cave
he in his
some nights both awaken, and call out
"*ou es tu?*"
not this night

tonight, as always, he stirs
he is awake
the night is full of his calling
of his smoke
of his fire
he calls to her, but she sleeps
she stirs, perhaps, just enough
to know that he is there
he thinks of her as she sleeps

he calls to her as she sleeps
"let my fire feed your thoughts"
"let my heart give you courage to do what
 you must do"
"let my smoke protect you from others"
"let my blood feed you and nurture you
 in your dark hours"
"let my strength nudge your hand as you write
 as you draw
 as you dwell in your cave"

"let my flames burn for you
    to inspire you
    to move you
    to give you light to see
    and strength to live"

and the dragon pauses
    listens
she is not there
but she is there
she has heard
a tiny wisp of smoke escapes from her
    as she sighs
and returns to sleep

this *minuit* they are not together
but they are the same
and as long as time counts
there will be dragon *minuits*

personal

In Memoriam

I've almost accepted the empty bed
The drain in the bathtub free of long black hair
Maybe there is just a twinge
Walking alone after dinner.
The plate goes directly into the dishwasher
    without pre-wash now
Without a pang of remorse.
I even leaf through the photo album
    and see her
Digging in her beloved garden
Wading in the creek up to her knees
Lying on the bed, waiting for me
And perhaps my eyes grow damp,
    nothing more.
But I broke down yesterday, at the rack
    in the foyer
Lifting the jacket from the old bronze hook
To reveal the leash, and the empty collar.

[for Abba]

Auld Acquaintance

After you left me, I couldn't work
Couldn't eat, couldn't sleep
I laid down on the sofa
[to the echoes of protesting cushions,
the house was so empty]
And drifted off...

And you stretched out beside me on the sofa
So warm and cozy
I felt the cushions yield under your body
[Dreams don't weigh much]
And you pressed yourself against me
And you whimpered, pleading
Your breast came alive in my hand
And I drifted back toward wakefulness
And I thought

And I thought

God, you're hairy!

Dogs always know when you're feeling really
          really down.
Abba knew...and she came to comfort me
Adding a wet tongue and doggie breath for good
measure

But I wish it had been you there.

Watch Me

He forbids me to write
My stories of horror
He fears my words of passion
May excite others toward me
I'm a wife, not a writer.
He says.

Watch me, I say, when he is gone.

He forbids me to think
He forbids me to dream

Watch me think.
Watch me dream.

darker

A Danger to Self and Others

The postal clerk eyed
her and the thick manila envelope
suspiciously
Shaking it
"Anything printed, liquid, hazardous—?"

"Don't spill it!" she screamed.

But it was too late.
Tiny silver droplets
rained onto the counter
each splash spreading
like a disease

The clerk covered his nose
and bent to read the droplets

". . . to right of them, cannon to . . ."
". . . ages hence: two roads diverged . . ."
". . . apples of the Moon, the golden . . ."
". . . I didn't know your eyes . . ."
". . . alone in the grip of a ghost . . ."
". . . are the stuffed men, leaning together . . ."
". . . build me straight, o worthy Master . . ."
". . . never send to know for whom the bell . . ."

The clerk had to
report her, of course
For violation of the
poetry control laws
After they came for her he
poured the contents of the envelope
into the toilet, then
carefully wiped up
every last drop on the counter
to protect the next customer

Spellchecker

You've seen the mistakes
Or read about them.
The so-called "acts of God."
Maybe you know someone
Who has been afflicted.
The infant with the cleft palate
Or only two fingers on the right hand
Or the flippers for feet.
Perhaps you think acne is the result
Of too much chocolate.
[But the scars can last forever].
Maybe someone you know
Has lost a clutch of loved ones
To an avalanche
Or a flood
Or a tornado
[You don't really think tornadoes
are phenomena of weather...do you?]
Have you suffered from indigestion?
Or a migraine?
Perhaps a hangnail?
Did you come home from work one day
With aching muscles, and sniffles,
    and a cough,
And blame it on the ventilation system?
Do you think leaders willingly
Order their followers
To commit acts of war?
Or atrocity?

Yes, you've seen all this
Or read about it.
But after each event,
Each storm, or indignation,
Or bout of acne or indigestion,
You never see the wraith in black
Who stands by the door of the labor room
While your wife gives birth.
Who stands at the top of the mountain
While the boulders of snow plummet.
Who points toward the border
And directs the traffic of armies.
Who watches, bemused, while you
Apply cosmetic foundation to your face
To hide the pits from your date.

Who cackles with glee each time
He reports back to his Dark Mistress:
"Well, that one worked."

First Fright

No matter how many Freddies they conjure
Or how many Jasons revive.
A sequel is only a sequel
The original template's alive.

You can make sausage links of intestines
Or fill up a sink with your barf
Norman's Mum can turn 'round to reveal
The skull that is under the scarf

Secret agents can break through your window
To drag you off into the night
And the taxman who comes every April
Is enough to give Old Drac a fright

Capillaries that course with your lifeblood
Can Rorschach the hallways with glee
["It's a shark. It's a breast. It's a beetle."]
And you see what you think you can see.

But nothing that teevee or movies
Can offer will fill you with dread
Like the monster who lurks in the closet
And the beastie who's under the bed

True Reflection

Impossible to gaze upon her
Without wanting her
Her face to the mirror, she sees there her
    naked skull
The self within herself
She is lovely beyond words, in her negligible
    negligee
Her skin incites touch
Even my touch, mine...skeleton that I am
    become
This past century
She does not know I exist in this house, not yet
She has closed her eyes
I approach from behind, hard as bone,
Fingers like dried bamboo wind chimes
My hands softly
Tenderly, gently
Glide down the slope of her breasts
To the unfurling camisole
And nudge the silken fabric down past
Her nipples
They come erect in my hands
    like thimbles in a pop-up sewing book
I press against her. She is warm, hot.
She is a vibrant "Yes!"
And she opens her eyes...and screams
Shrieks
Writhes
In the mirror I see, behind her skull
A very handsome man.

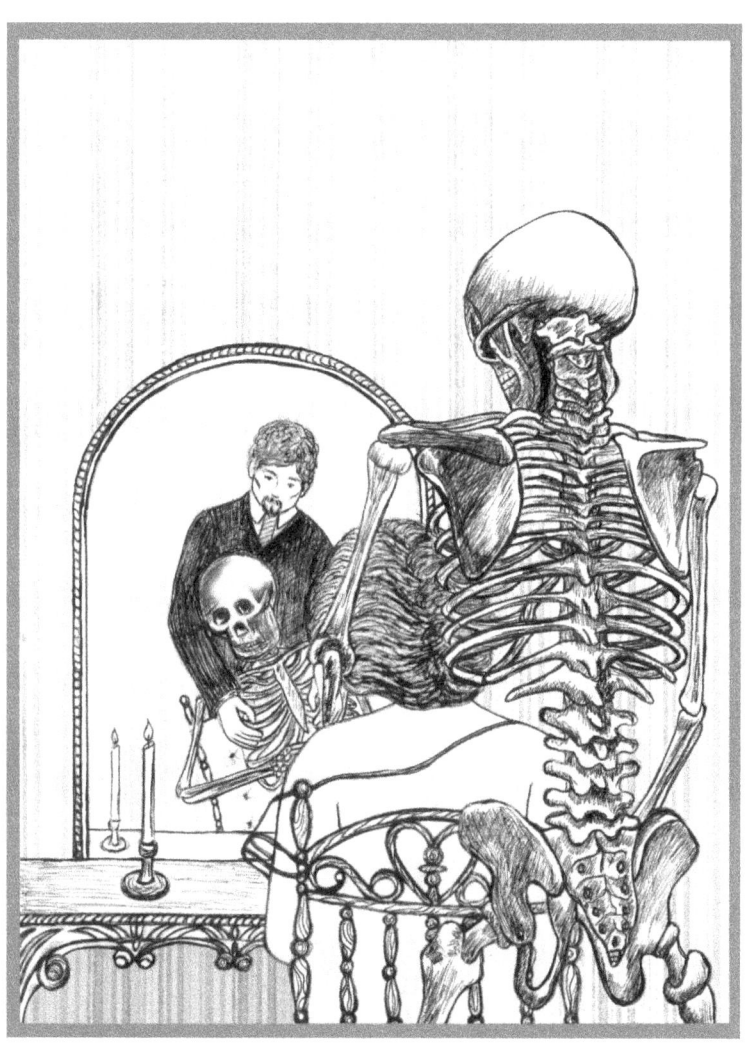

Purrifurry

I know he's out there, jealous now
I won't let him back in
[lock the doors, check the windows...
         did I miss one?]
They like to lie where it's warm
Creeping up on the bed while you sleep
Curling up beside your face...or on it
And you can't breathe
They don't do that on purpose...do they?
I can't take the chance, not now
Not with the new baby in the house

[Did I check the cellar window?
I can't remember...
I don't get much sleep,
with Caitlin crying every two hours
...and she's due to cry any minute now.
At least she is a regular feeder.
Every other hour, on the hour.
Ten twelve two and four.
...any minute now]

How he hated that day I came home
The reduced attention,
the altered feeding times
Not allowing him to curl up on my lap
While I watched "Oprah."
I love him, but...he'll be okay outside.
I've put the litter box on the porch
And the little tub of 9 Lives

And I'll say hi to him in the morning.
After a good night's sleep.
Hmm...and Caitlin hasn't cried yet...
Maybe this time she'll sleep
      through the night.

Me That Was

No friends, only competitors
No sunrises

Romantic walks at night in the park
do not end well

Nightly drudgery
over and over,
forever

I could . . .
or I could . . .
But no matter what I do
the song, as they say,
remains the same

I stare for hours at a faded photograph
Mom and Dad, Billy & me . . .
. . . *sigh*

Bringing Sally Back

She lay there in the coffin,
and her lips were turning blue.
The priest and doctor claimed that
there was nothing they could do.
"Your Sally has moved on
but you will see her by and by."
The mourners passed in order
one by one to say goodbye.

Her hands were clasped upon her
on the gown beneath her breasts,
Her fingers clutched a crimson rose,
the kind that she loved best.
When Gramma stopped and pulled
a little petal, Sally sighed.
And Mamma bent down close
and shed a tear that quickly dried.

Then sister Nell who never ever
walked around by day
Emerged from corner shadows
for she had something to say.
Her voice was soft and gentle
though the words she spoke were tart,
Like berries not yet ripened.
Sally gave a little start.

We couldn't hear Nell's words, of course,
but we knew what they meant.
And when our Poppa closed the lid,
he left a little vent.
The time had come for us to
share our mem'ries at the wake.
For sev'ral hours we laughed and wept
without a single break.

The funeral procession was now
ready to start out.
The driver of the hearse could
not be found a'ywhere about.
The tail of his black tux was
dangling from the coffin lid.
But none of us dared check to
find out just what Sally did.

We fled the scene. Now idling cars
still wait under the sun.
We knew what Gram and Momma
and our sister Nell had done.
Each poem tells a story true,
and so I write this verse.
If you think Sally's dead, then *you*
can ride inside the hearse.

Size 15W Should Do It
[after George Orwell]

Do not adjust your media
Do not adjust your TV,
      your smart phone,
Your tablet, your Twitter
We control the horizontal
We control the vertical
We control the input
We tell you what to think
We tell you how to think
We tell you when to think
If you have a thought, or an idea,
It comes from us
Not from you
There is no opposition
If you think there is opposition
It is because we told you to think
There is opposition
We are your Emmanuel Goldstein
There is no Emmanuel Goldstein
You only think there is
Because we told you to think there is
Soon enough we will tell you
Not to think there is
And you will not think there is
You will not think
Unless we tell you to think
What to think

How to think
When to think
This does not bother you
If you think it bothers you
It is because we told you to think
That it bothers you
We control your emotional responses
We tell you how to behave
We tell you what to buy
We tell you whom to love
We tell you whom to hate
We tell you what to fear
If you think you do not love or hate
       or fear
It is because we tell you
Not to love or hate or fear
When we want you to buy
We tell you to buy
And you buy
When we want you to hate
We tell you to hate
We tell you whom to hate
And you hate
When we want you to love
We tell you to love
We tell you whom to love
And you love
When we want you to fear
We tell you to fear
We tell you what to fear
And you are terrified

We control your emotions
We tell you to riot
We tell you to burn
We tell you to destroy
We tell you to kill
We tell you these things
Because they require no thought
We do not want you to think
Unless we tell you to think
What to think
How to think
When to think
You think your thoughts are yours
If we tell you to think they are yours
You do not ask where they came from
Because we do not tell you to ask
You do not consider the media
The news reports
The advertisements
The TV programs
The movies
The song lyrics
The classrooms
Your thoughts are not your thoughts
They are our thoughts
We tell you what to watch
We tell you why you should watch it
We tell you what to listen to
We tell you why you should listen to it
We tell you these programs
These advertisements

These news reports
These songs
These movies
These classes
Are good
Our thoughts to your thoughts
We are your Vulcan mind meld
We are your educators
We teach you the same thoughts
Because you all think
The same way
You are in lockstep
Even your opposition
Is in lockstep
That is because we teach you
The same thoughts
The same emotional responses
We teach you this on TV
We teach you this in movies
We teach you this in social media
We teach you this in the classroom
If you do not think you are in lockstep
It is because we tell you to think
You are not in lockstep
Soon enough we will tell you
To think in lockstep
And you will think in lockstep
With everyone else
In the meantime
Do not adjust your media
If we want you to adjust your media

We will tell you
You are a bazillion chickens
With but one head
With but one thought
Soon enough
When we are ready
We will decapitate you
And move on to the next generation

minimalist

scifaiku

hatch ajar
decomposing puddles on the deck
stale echoes of screams

perfect poem
no words
telempathic

on . . . off . . . on . . . off
strobe light
Weena harassing Morlocks

starlight, star bright
8½ minutes left
just enough time, babe

tanka

The Portal on the Third Day

on the third day the portal closed
between your world and mine
like a camera lens
your glistening eyes
longing . . .

Tanka

fall of Earth
controlled numbers
human mating season
alien reproduction permit
rose-scented sheets

Featured Poet
Scifaikuest August 2008

Ingsoc:
global warming
cultural diversity
how many fingers

robot baby
thumb in mouth
short circuit

core sample
between silt and ash
styro-popcorn

hot gas cloud
new stars from old
second chances

lost colony of Mars
helmet faceplates touching
last kiss

night shift city beat
composing obituaries
did that shadow just move?

The Blob—
an amoeba
on steroids

after the masquerade
the costume—
au naturelle

nuclear winter
light from the glacier
is not a reflection

thunderstorm at night
power outage
the curtain moves . . .

natives terrified
stenciled on robot lander:
"we come in peace"

AI dying
terminals terminating
. . . "what are you doing, Dave?"

tanka:

suicide victim
pile of string
Pinocchio despondent
beside his hand
a pair of scissors

tanka:

volcano on Io
great plumes of sulfur
an astronaut with a
section of loading ramp . . .
surf's up!

haibun: when life gives you lemons

While in orbit around Io he went EVA to realign a reflector dish, his great white suit gleaming in the light reflected up from Jupiter. He wished there were someone with him in the satellite observation post, someone to talk with and assist, but there had come up a temporary shortage of personnel. Still, he had only twenty three days to go before the relief arrived.

When he had finished realigning the dish, he engaged his suit thruster jets to take him aft of the satellite so that he could examine the particulate sensor that was accumulating data from the latest eruption of yellow ash from the surface of Io. Too late he noticed that he had inadvertently become untethered. In a desperate and unsuccessful grab for the tether's end buckle with his thickly mittened hand, he brushed against the dial that controlled the thruster jets, setting it almost to maximum. By the time he recovered from that blunder, he was several kilometers away, his thruster fuel exhausted, and his momentum still carrying him away from the observation post.

   eruption of sulfur volcano
   Jupiter-rise beyond Io
   a view to die for

haibun: &%$#ing Einstein

He had spent his childhood and adolescence gazing at the stars and galaxies, studying the mythologies from which they had been named, and dreaming of one day traveling to them, to see what was out there. That day arrived, and he was sent forth at nearly the speed of light toward a star with a possible Earth-twin.

When he returned he had aged thirty years, but the Earth had aged three million. His beloved constellations, the blaze marks for his trail to the stars, were changed or gone forever, and he felt a loneliness that came not from the lack of a companion but from the loss of his personal compass.

    time dilation
    Orion
    is now Oriona

oddments

My Grandfather's Corpse
[sung to the tune of 'My Grandfather's Clock']

My grandfather's corpse was too large
    for the shelf
So it stayed in the freezer downstairs
If you wanted a snack you could go help
    yourself
And hack off chunks with nary a care

He was large, he was mean, and he loved to
    vent his spleen
And he'd beat us until we all cried
But we've not missed a meal from his head
    to his heel
Since the old man died.

His frozen remains cause no more aches
    and pains
And his whip hangs so limp from the door
And the canes he applied to our tender
    backsides
Now lie splintered in dust on the floor

Now his legs and his arms cause nobody
    any harm
Now it's him that is prodded and poked
And antacids help pass all our digestive gas
Since the old man croaked.

Oh . . .
He was big, he was tall, and he loved to make us bawl
So he'd beat us until we all cried
But we've not missed a meal from his head to his heel
Since the old man died.

Acknowledgements

The following poems were first published as indicated:

Auld Acquaintance: Expressions Newsletter, November 2001
Black Dragon: The Modern Art Cave, January 2003
A Danger to Self and Others: Star*Line, July 2007
Evolution: The Fifth Di..., October 2001
First Fright: Rogue Worlds, July 2002
The Garden Party: The Martian Wave, November 2001
In Memoriam: Expressions Newsletter, May 2002
Itinerant: Aoife's Kiss, March 2004
My Grandfather's Corpse: Disturbed Digest, March 2016
Not One of Us: Sex and the Single Alien, May 2002
The Portal of the Third Day: Tales from the Moonlit Path, January 2006
Purrifurry: Bare Bone #4, September 2003
Spellchecker: Naked Snake Online, September 2003
Tanka 'fall of Earth': Scifaikuest May 2005
True Reflection: Mirrors in Flame, July 2003
Why the Solar System Really Lost Its Tenth Planet: The Martian Wave, March 2001

A Wolf to Guard the Door
By Tyree Campbell

Mobs rule!

Societies around the globe have fallen apart, as more things go wrong than can be counted. Furious mobs riot, loot, torch, and slaughter. Others quietly hoard and hide, and pray. Communications function intermittently. Electromagnetic pulses damage electronics and render many vehicles useless. Soldiers and police leave their jobs to spend the last moments with their families.

One small and desperate group from the U.S. heads for the sparsely-populated and undesirable Pyrenees, hoping to be left alone. But their animosities make them a microcosm of society's breakdown. Blake's wife was butchered by Muslims. Nouh, a Boston cabbie, is a Muslim. Nollaig has just given birth and slows the group's progress. Jameela hates white folks. Addison Temple thinks he should be in charge because he has money. Tonya doesn't care for men. Miller Sinclair, an ex-Marine, is running out of patience, and she has a loaded pistol. Adriana is a Romani, her people driven out by the French. And teenager Derek Post is oblivious to everything but his GameBoy.

They've all crowded into Blake's SUV. Maybe the onrushing tsunami won't reach them. Maybe their vehicle won't run out of gas. Maybe they'll make it to the mountains.

This is the way the world ends...and might begin again...if they don't kill each other first.

www.hiraethsffh.com/product-page/a-wolf-to-guard-the-door-by-tyree-campbell

www.ingramcontent.com/pod-product-compliance
Lightning Source LLC
LaVergne TN
LVHW012033060526
838201LV00061B/4589